music for Funeral & Remembrance Services for manuals

EDITED & ARRANGED BY

C. H. TREVOR

ELKIN

Order No: NOV 262751

EDITORIAL NOTE

Although the pieces in this book have suggestions for registration on an organ of two (and sometimes three) manuals, they can be played effectively on a one-manual instrument with appropriate stops. The pedals can be used at the player's discretion. When the dynamics only are given, the choice of registration is left to the player.

As stops with the same names do not always produce the same effect on different organs, other registrations should be used if those suggested are not effective or suitable on any particular instrument. The directions for registration in brackets may be used or not at the player's discretion.

If the organ is an unenclosed one-manual, the dynamics should be ignored except where it is possible to change the registration without interrupting the flow of the music.

Most of the pieces in this book are suitable for use on other occasions.

Certain sections and repeats may be omitted if a piece is found to be too long for the required time.

C. H. T.

CONTENTS

TWO INTERLUDES

Christian Georg Höpner
(1799—1860)

Sw. Diapason 8. (or Ch. Flutes 8. 4.)

Moderato

No. 1.

Johann Christian Heinrich Rinck
(1770—1846)

Sw. soft 8.

Lento espressivo

No. 2.

AIR

Sw. (or Ch.) soft 8.

Spohr
(1784—1859)

EQUALE

Sw. Diapason 8. (box closed)

Beethoven
(1770—1827)

This piece, written for four trombones, was performed at the composer's funeral.

"Christus, der ist mein Leben"
★No. 1. Chorale

Diapason 8.

Melody by
Melchior Vulpius
(1560 – 1615)

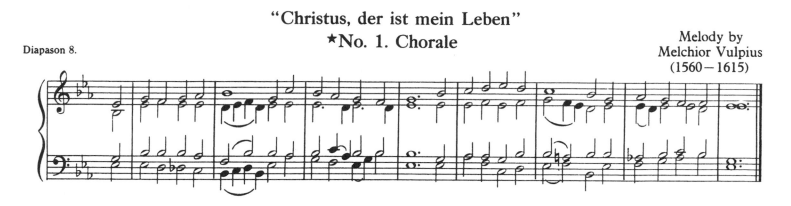

No. 2. Duo. Chorale in the Soprano

R.H. Sw. Oboe 8.
L.H. Ch. soft 8. 4. (or Gt. soft 8.)
[or Flutes 8. 4. both hands.]

Johann Gottlob Töpfer
(1791 – 1870)

No. 3. Chorale in the Soprano

Sw. Diapason 8.

Gustav Merkel
(1827 – 1885)

★This melody is sung to the words, "My soul there is a country
Far beyond the stars".

No. 4. Chorale in the Soprano

Johann Pachelbel
(1653—1706)

Gt. Dulciana 8. Flute 4. (or Sw. soft 8.)

Andantino

No. 5. Chorale in the Bass

Merkel

R.H. Sw. Diapason 8.
L.H. Gt. Diapason 8.

Andante

rall.

No. 6. Chorale in the Soprano

Pachelbel

Ch. Flutes 8. 4. (or Sw. soft 8.)

Tranquillo

No. 7. Chorale in the Soprano

Ch. (or Sw.) soft 8.

Pachelbel

Lento assai

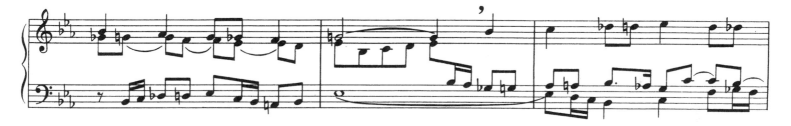

No. 8. Chorale

Diapason 8.

Each of the above eight items can be played with the same registration e.g.
Flute(s) 8. (4.) or soft Diapason 8.

LAMENTO

Justin Heinrich Knecht
(1752—1817)

Sw. soft 8.

Lento espressivo

MARCIA RELIGIOSA
(from "Alceste")

Gluck
(1714—1787)

Gt.
Sw. } Diapason 8.

Moderato

If preferred, each section can be played on the Great and repeated on the Swell.

"O REST IN THE LORD"
(from "Elijah")

Mendelssohn
(1809 – 1847)

Sw. soft 8.

TWO PIECES

César Franck
(1822—1890)

No. 1. Epitaphe

Sw. soft 8.

No. 2. Consolation

Sw. Diapason 8.

MARCHE FUNÈBRE
(from Sonata Op. 35)

Gt. *f*
Sw. *p*
Sw. to Gt.

Chopin
(1810 — 1849)

*If preferred, this section can be played with both hands on soft Swell 8.

Chorale prelude, "Durch Adams fall ist ganz verderbt"

Gt. Diapason(s) 8. (4.)

J. S. Bach
(1685 — 1750)

Pièce funèbre

Léon Boëllmann
(1862 – 1897)

If preferred, this piece can be played on the Swell throughout.

FUNERAL MARCH
(from Sonata Op. 26)

Beethoven
(1770 — 1827)

If the observance of the dynamics is not practicable on any particular instrument, the suggested registration —or other registration which the player considers suitable—can be used throughout. If the organ is an unenclosed one—manual, the piece can be played on Diapason(s) 8. (4.) throughout or changes made at convenient places by hand if other means are not available.

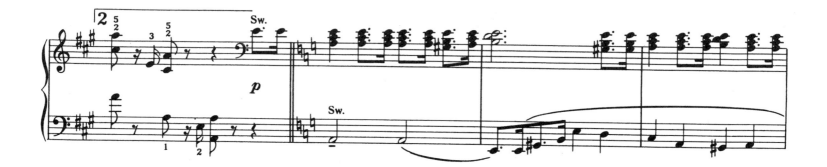

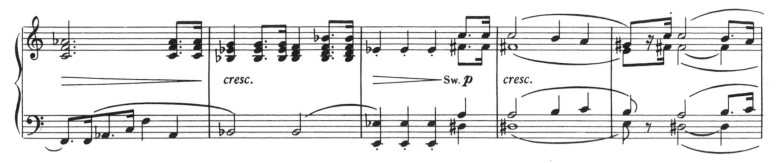

"AVE VERUM"

Sw. Diapason 8. (box closed)

Mozart
(1756—1791)

TWO PIECES

Gt. (or Ch.) Flute 8.
Sw. soft 8.

Henry Purcell
(1658—1695)

No. 1. Sarabande

No. 2. Adagio
(from "The Golden Sonata")

Sw. Diapason 8.

Andante cantabile
(from String Quartet Op. 11)

Solo. Gt. (or Ch.) solo stop 8.
Sw. soft 8. (box slightly open.)

Tchaikovsky
(1840—1893)

If preferred, this piece can be played on one manual throughout.

FUNERAL MARCH
(adapted from Op. 62, No. 3)

Mendelssohn
(1809—1847)

This piece, arranged for wind band by Moscheles, was played in the procession at the composer's funeral.

Air, "Bist du bei mir"

Gt.⎫
Sw.⎬ soft 8.
Sw. to Gt.

J. S. Bach
(1685 — 1750)

Andante sostenuto

If preferred, this piece can be played on the Swell throughout.

TWO PRELUDES

R.H. Ch. (or Gt.) solo stop 8.
L.H. Sw. soft 8.

In E minor (Op. 28, No. 4.)

Chopin
(1810—1849)

This piece can be played with both hands on one manual.
If the R.H. part is played on the Great, the Swell should be coupled.
If the Choir is unenclosed, the Swell should be coupled.

In C minor (Op. 28, No. 20)

Gt.
Sw.(open)} Diapason 8.

THREE PIECES

No. 1. Dead March
(from "Saul")

Handel
(1685 — 1759)

No. 2. "I know that my Redeemer liveth"
(from "Messiah")

Gt. } 8.
Sw. }
Sw. to Gt.

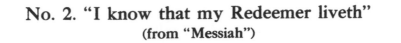

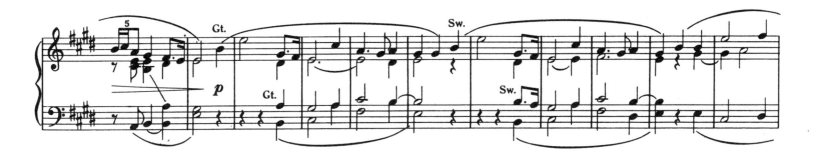

If preferred, this piece can be played on the Swell throughout.

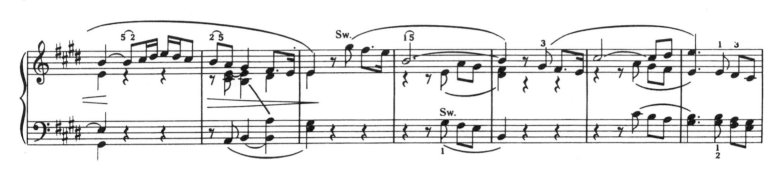

No 3. Minuet
(from "Berenice")

Gt.
Sw. } soft 8.
Sw. to Gt.

If preferred, this piece can be played on one manual throughout.